THE FESTIVAL OF WILD ORCHID

ACKNOWLEDGEMENTS

Some of the poems in this anthology have appeared in various forms in the following journals and anthologies: *Caribbean Writer*; *BIM*; *Journal of Caribbean Literatures*; *Calabash: a Journal of Caribbean Arts and Letters*; *Caribbean Quarterly*; the Calabash poetry workshop anthology, *So Much Things to Say*; WiSPA's anthology, *Motherlogue*; the Black Londoners' Haiti Anthology, *A Lime Jewel*; the *Pittsburg Quarterly* online; and the *Jamaica Gleaner* and the *Jamaica Observer*.

Special thank you to Kwame Dawes, Jeremy Poynting, Hannah Bannister and the rest of the Peepal Tree Press crew, who made this book happen!

Thank you to Dr. Clinton Hutton the photographer and artist; to my mentors living in this island – namely Earl McKenzie, Eddie Baugh and Mervyn Morris. The latter two's classes at UWI, alongside Victor Chang's and Esther Tyson's ('A' level high school English teacher) were the soil in which the seed was sown. Thank you, too, Wayne Brown, for the time to you gave me. Thank you Neville for being the bouncing board for my poems, a good listener, with a keen ear. And for Kayla (and you too Nev.) for being my always-willing audience. Thank you: Safiya Sinclair for your genuine friendship since our meeting at the Workshop Retreat years ago and Cecil Gray whose airmailed publications are gratefully read.

Thank you poets, living and dead, whom I've read and who've influenced me.

THE FESTIVAL OF WILD ORCHID

ANN-MARGARET LIM

PEEPAL TREE

First published in Great Britain in 2012
Peepal Tree Press Ltd
17 King's Avenue
Leeds LS6 1QS
UK

ISBN 13: 9781845232016

Supported by
ARTS COUNCIL
ENGLAND

For the poets who've inspired me and for my family –
Neville and Kayla, and the rest.

CONTENTS

III

I

...here as in other times I come forth
to sing or to die: here I begin
— Pablo Neruda "Puerto Rico, Puerto Pobre"

JOURNEY

I

She crossed over from the changing mountains
when Mou was the bad dragon and they fled
on a big ship to an island.

She lost her tonsils on the ship,
dug them out with two chopsticks,
and gargled with the ocean at 16.

She married a Jamaican Chinaman
and twelve feet ran up the wooden steps
of a downtown house and shop.

She spat hot Jamaican words from the counter
to the downtown man standing in the shop
of the damn mean Chinaman and his *industry.*

Oh, why does the earth plunge into darkness?
His pudginess and a sky-rocketing pressure took him
when the mirrors still sat behind books and a bench.

And the old mountains of China walked into the dream
of the girl in exile, shipped from the red commune
to this blue island of salt and single mothers.

II

On her way over to her first grandson,
she heard the fearful whispers
of lights fidgeting in the night sky,
and screams twisted her head
on the hospital wall.

Years on, the sun was the fidgeting light
when he passed from them
into the land of photographs.

III

I remember some things, I don't remember them all.
I remember the old woman who was always sick
and the old man and the quarrels they had
in the yard where they say I lived.
And for what reason I remember
the pipe and the carbolic,
I don't know,
but I remember when at almost four
I met the Chinese woman whose eyes are the beacons
in my life, the gentle owl who watches
and folds me in her homely wings.

IV

Sitting in the plane with a daughter beside her
– the one who gave up art for the office –
she wonders about her boy – the last one
who taught her to read English and to write it;
the one whose wife was a Jamaican girl
who loved him in that *same* gentle way;

Sitting in the plane, anxious to unload
and run to her son,
she examines the memories, stories
of her family,
to find what wrong was done the dragon
for it to turn and curse the bloodline
to an exile from land and
a disposition to widowhood.

V

Japo, I don't sleep so good since you're away.
How's your son?

THE DARKENING

It will eat off my jaw,
this thing that keeps creeping in.
It sprung from him – the brown boy
who hated a mother
and a father
who put him on a ship to China.

"They sent me away to be a slave
– a brown boy in a yellow country."

They say Bruce Lee's line is cursed;
a dragon followed him from Mainland
and ate his son.
My father's heritage is a darkening that grips the skin,
seeping the black night in.

But there's one last hope for light –
this tending of the verse that springs
from my father who strummed banjo strings,
blew into his harmonica
and sang Chinese opera.

THE FESTIVAL OF WILD ORCHID

I

It was death
riding the ocean in a tomb of bodies;
so she howled an ancestor-waking howl

to her grandmother spirit in the trees, who,
stripped bare, begged the West Indies
to fit her granddaughter with wild orchid
leaves and the hardiness of a tree.

II

A tree stands bare, naked
like the first African woman
to stand on this island,
with a swelling ocean for a tongue
and a cry
that stripped the trees of all the leaves.

Mark it!
It is the Festival of Wild Orchid.

GIRLS SCHOOL, ST. ANDREW

For Esther Tyson

It was girls in cliques – the politics of skin and kin,
a dragon teacher who said it was your kinky hair
that made it hard to remember the use of the equator.

Girls with the night wind in their throats traded it
for a caged bird; no words at all.
Only the pretty – the invisible insignia on the left breast.

The A-line dress is not for fat girls.
Your black bottoms uneven the skirt.

But for one pixie woman who took them to the land
where words commandeered imagination,
the girls of the class would have faded, 'specially this one.

OLD VIRGIN

Had this teacher once, she shouted,
"Ladies cross their feet at the ankles!"
when I crossed mine at the knees.

Bet she never knew what she did
with her classroom tactics, like the old pirates,
identifying *me* as bad!

Bet she never knew she sowed this woman
who sees bamboo-leaf ballerinas in the wind;
this woman who collects pieces of the sea

– driftwood, pebbles, coral, shells
and stores them beside her;
this woman walking, talking to her soul;

this woman stricken by the sight of a tree
that never drank the rain,
a tree dying upward from its roots.

INSOMNIA

Sometimes the river is my mother,
sometimes it's the moon.
Then I find sweet
despair in the dark folds
of a woman who knows
the stillness,
the horror of night.

And my eyes fix to the unblinking
face that guards the night;
I don't let go her gaze
until the lunging sun jabs the blanket

— the everyday rehearsal
for the last night.

When the last night comes,
I will have one mother.
She will be the moon.

SYLVIA

Friend, far from the world with its grey
wizards and witches who carve trenches
till the human soul is a sieve
and the blood leaves,
tell me, what's it like?

Do diamond-studded butterflies
swarm a country cottage where you rest
your pretty head to dream a dream
as real, unreal, as you, woman at thirty?

Does the geranium wake all day, all night?
Do you see a poppy blooming in October?
Does your lover ever come home?
Do you write free verses,
musing under a willow tree with coconut wafers
and paint happy thoughts
of you and the chubby ones?

Do you leaf through the greats,
written, not yet written,
argue at night with the gods,
an equal philosopher?
Are heaven and earth one wonderland?

Here, nothing works for the flower girl.
Here, they push their toes into square shoes,
eat grey, and fear the people
who live, like you, by the rainbow.

EDNA

The first time I went to Nomdmi
I took some shrubs
and stuck them in my grandmother's garden;
she loves flowers like you did,
or, do you still – in that world?

I should've asked the air for them,
before I plucked the yellow faces,
but I thanked you in whisper
as we tucked them in a new bed.
And I told my grandmother the things I saw –
the pine tree you moulded a love seat in.

I told her of the azaleas;
the rose bed;
the driveway that was a walk
in the woods littered with pine-cones
like an English scene
in the Blue Mountains
– your summer retreat
from Drumblair.

I told her of the pictures.
"I saw Michael's rippled chest
and that handsome smugness
holding a swimmer's trophy.
And Grandma, they looked happy
– two simple people nestled on a step."

I find myself standing in your study again,
the workshop really, where I imagine
you shaped the heads of horses
and wooden rainbows,

sometime after you woke
and opened the window out,
to a Blue Mountain morning.

GARDENING

There's the plantain he planted
last summer that's flourishing
and there's the stunted cane and okra I planted
– with ants on the cane stalk and no okra.

But there are my flowers…
The buttercups and marigolds are sweet
and yellow. There's the French hibiscus,
ixoras – my humming bird seducers,

and although its name is so painful,
the rose-pink petals of the crown of thorns are graceful.
Plus I can't wait to smell the ginger lilies'
perfume, or the gift of the night-blooming cereus.

And though they say the angel's trumpets are poisonous
to the skin, I'll take my chances,
since I've messed with the celestial before
and, like the infamous one, my kingdom is this earth

that I dig with fingers and a fork
to stick in it the stem or root of a poinsettia
in spring, after the Magi season
when its leaves are red and trembling.

And while six-fingered Heather whispers
secrets to the ferns and busy Lizzie blushes,
the wandering Jew, who has no time for secrets,
is regenerating in my basket,

like Moses in the cradle, there
by the column; they thrive
even while in the exile of my garden
in Red Hills, Jamaica.

And while I see that prayer plants lose their stripes
to the sun and to the rain,
that the leaves of the caladium are speckled hearts,
I hope my lucky bamboo is just that.

RESTAURATEUR

Remember last year?
You wanted lignum vitae leaves
to run the flies from your restaurant.

I'm sitting under the tree.
There are no flies, just a lonesome bee
that the wind whirls in cyclones.

The sun burns memories
into dry leaves at my feet.
The goats eat toasted grass.

If I give you an altar of burnt meat,
would the flies still live with you
at the restaurant?

But time retrenches the cast of last year
when you, the lignum vitae leaves
and the restaurant mattered.

CRAB

When she had looked away

he came up from a hole in the beach,
dug his eyes into her well and
read every line –

a crab in the skin.

The mole was the mountain;
the girl, the fingered eye.

The world spins.
Then, the blackness.

DREAMS

I

The Cat

The she-cat's teeth sank into her skin.
She jerked the cat, but it held.
She woke with the cat on her mind.

Next twilight she dreamt a man
with a cat face,
with tomcat pupils fixed on her.

II

Nymph

At night she soars in dream to
a great assurance of love
felt in the bone – happiness
that fills in, wells over, from Jove!

At night she circles in dream for
a world, a universe to love,
a man to give everything –
up to the last ti dum ti dum

of blood pounding her spring.

SEEING GOD

Elegy for Sylvia Plath

...is being seized up,
every bit parcelled off
to the ripple that is
a voice in the morning,
a voice that weaves through all
the tides of the hidden
to plug sound waves
of the first known, now unknown,
into your bone;

...is being stitched to the gaze
that sees beyond every horizon
and every façade of the end
to the never beginning and never ending;

...is being stapled to the cool breeze
that is a voice in the evening
on which you ride,
sprinkling
the dust of poems.

LOVE NOTES IN WATER

I

No sound but the waves;
a cay and its coconuts;
a dark sea as warm as breath;
black pebbles scuttling up;
black pebbles washing back.

And these two, cradled
by the tide, in each other.

No sound but the waves…

II

Let's go to Caymanas –
I'll have sprat or some other fish
and listen to the music –
or maybe not.
I'll just listen to the music
and watch you and the water –
or, maybe I won't do that.
I'll wash your feet in the water,
the nape of your neck,
the small of your back…

SUNDAY

with hands in her pockets
like a soul at gaze on the beach

flicking sand with her feet,
walks easy;

she sits on the bench,
hears the sigh in the robin's nest;

sees the gull disappear into
the blue crease of sea and sky

lazy as the days of summer
when his love grew deeper.

GIVE ME A GOD

but silent, absorbed and on his knees
as men adore God at the altar, as I love you
don't blind yourself, you'll not be loved like that.
Robert Lowell, "Will Not Come Back"

You say none will ever love me like this,
the way you do, silent, absorbed, on your knees.
I say, I've had enough glibness to fill
all the kitchen-counter romance novels.
I don't need someone on his knees sounding
his brazen love to me; it's trite, and glows
like tinsel town, it's just an overload.
Give me a god like the sea or gloomy clouds
to love; the folding, unfolding mountains
to search, to comprehend, to serenade,
to sow golden marigolds on, and
a spring to dip my careless feet.
Oh give me the woods to run to, away
from all this clanging of men's mortal love.

THE CAVE

It was Negril's west end
and a slower track.
Always the sea, always
the cliffs and a long sunset,

and Patrick the masseur
goading us to dive into
the cave outside our room,
first thing at sunrise.

We peered into the deep blue
cave the day we came,
but spent our morning in
the blue room with coconut

incense and a stone-cut bed.
Now, in memory,
the blue of our room was like the sea
that spread to the horizon,

the blue canvas of the sky
that turned grey when storms threatened —
like this hurricane
we're in, with no light, with only

a radio, while outside the white wind
crashes down the bananas, howling.

INHERITANCE

for my unborn

Here on earth you will learn
there are no binary systems,
no two moons, no two suns,
no twin trees rising from one root.
What there is,
the universe roars in me,
is loneliness.

My mother left me this.

The first leaving keeps rehearsing
in my head. And as you grow in me
I fear what you will find here,
but know:

I won't be leaving you.

BABY & THE BALL

It was just a ball in the air, but
by the way baby cheered you'd
think I'd put on a show
like a clown in a big red bow,
with a sidekick and a water gun,
who'd round and round a circle run –
but it was just a ball,
I'd now and then let fall,
though you'd think it was some feat
like walking upside down; through teeth
singing, *Oh the grand old duke...*
Wasn't a parachute
with a GI Jane,
or the first drops of rain
why my baby squealed
and laughed and pealed –
it was just a ball
I bounced on the wall,
but her mirth was so complete
I marvelled at the feet
of my baby – in awe,
goggle-eyed, enthralled;
a role reversed:
I, the babe,
she the bouncing ball.

FIXING THE MOON

Moon!
Moon! Look! –
My twenty-one month-old dishevels evening
to name the moon.
And I, like a bovine creature,
could only obey, and *look*
at the full moon, with wide, brimming eyes
and at my daughter
fixing the moon with a finger.

A LESSON FOR THIS FRIDAY

Heredity of cruelty everywhere,
And everywhere the frocks of summer torn
− Derek Walcott "A Lesson for this Sunday"

Eyes locked into mine
you crushed the tiny army of ants
with a foot I hadn't realised
had already known the thrill,
the pleasure of the kill.

You crushed the tiny army of ants
delivering a dead bee to their storehouse,
and stared square at me:

Look, this I've learnt
these 700 odd days from the womb!

And knowing Walcott's fear
and near nausea,
I sink to think that my daughter
is belonging to this world.

FOR THE MOTHER AND CHILD

Blood seeped down
into the veins of our Earth

and I held my child and cried

for a mother and child
woke that Tuesday to die.

I held my child and cried
for the mother and child in Haiti;

for the memory of Toussaint,
Dessalines;

for the Haitians never mentioned in the books;
for the Haitian with the monkey on his back.

Pat Robertson (and the others), tell me, if you know,
why was the black man's God a devil?

Why was there a price
for the air you breathe in Haiti?

Blood seeped down
into the veins of our Earth

and I held my child and cried.

II

Progress is history's dirty joke.
Ask that sad green island getting nearer.
– Derek Walcott, "The Schooner Flight"

BY THE BROOK

The trees reach to touch the sky;
there are blossoms
and the birdsong never dies.

You don't need shoes
to walk with azaleas,
to sit on a rock by the brook
where the air is spiced with wild ginger lilies,
April mango blossoms
and the green wax of cocoa leaves;

to listen to the water,
a stir of youth one minute,
a woman like the moon,
rotund and knowing, the next.

TAINO OF RED HILLS

The story goes: they were blasting the hill
and found you – three Taino skeletons –
mother, father, child, huddled

like a family facing a tsunami;
like a family about to be hacked,
mown down by a fleet
of genocidal conquistadors.

They excavated you, stored you in a museum,
but your lives lived here on this hill
can't be raked away like the leaves
of my Julie mango tree.

When evening comes with the dying sun
I think of your evenings after the pepper pot,
catching the breeze on a hammock.

When the woodpecker pecks some hollow tree
at sunrise, I think of your mornings
of countless birds in these hills
when the hills were young.

When I drive through the short-cuts of the hill,
down to the river, to the sea,
I imagine your journeys downhill
to river, to sea for turtles, for fish.

When I look at my dog reddened by the soil
of this hill, I construct a story

of bloodletting.

AFTER THE DROWNING

When my car eats up Palisadoes
I think, "What if an earthquake happened here?
It would come swimming up,
like the whale devouring Jonah,
and I would try to outdrive it!"

And what of the people taken in
by the sea I swear crouches ever
closer, each time I navigate Palisadoes.

Their last thoughts would come
crashing, as death – a giant hand of
sea – unfurls on them.

It's crippling
after the adrenaline runs out
and there's nothing –
you die from that.

And I see them. They walk silently
among the living, mouths
stitched into Os
of terror and drowning.

AND IT DON'T HAVE TO BE GOOD FRIDAY NOON

They come up from the Rio Cobre
– the waving gallery –
with words from their lips that buzz
like a hundred crickets,
a million zephyrs in the air.

And some who hear
the words sharp in their ear
and see the hands that wave,
release the wheel to go home
under the Flat Bridge.

THE CLIFF

It wasn't a gentle slope like the one
I see through these windows
where yellow Xs were taped on
for hurricanes that didn't come;
it was a cliff you'd shun
if there wasn't the fame tacked on
by two lovers who leapt
from unbearably separate lives
to ghosts who strived
with what life denied them,
when they owned nothing:

not dreams,
not themselves,
not a pen

like this one, now painting a cliff
terrible in height, drenched in grief
and the knowledge that night dwells
in every tomorrow,
though the sea washes all things.

POOR PEOPLE COUNTRY

I

No voltage
so the wooden house with babies
bun from de candle.

II

Damian has the ringworms again
– dis time in 'im face.

III

You pardon the madman in his SUV
threatening to bulldoze you with a swerve:
'cause de potholes dem BIG!

IV

You've always heard shit's in the drinking water,
fi dem who have it.
You've heard, too, guns in the night and in the day,
no matta whey yu live.
And no matter who you are, you've known
somebody tek down by the gun;
somebody beat up by 'ar man.

V

In this land of the bad man, schools are ganglands
and teachers are preys who've lost all worth.
Sometimes when a policeman dies, you hear rumours.

VI

We're all carrying water baskets;
big houses on hills have empty cupboards,
empty plates.

VII

Government makes its noise about this and that,
but doan aks question, yu dumb Quashee,
fin' some tyres, old furniture,
an' bun Babylon/Rome down
in de middle ah dem govanment road.

HAVE NO SEAT IN LEGBA COUNTRY
For Derek Walcott

> *...Find a name*
> *for that look on the faces*
> *of the electorate. Tell me*
> *how it all happened, and why*
> *I said nothing.*
> — Derek Walcott, "Parades, Parades"

You said nothing, for you walked their footways,
told the same sky goodnight with the same moon
dangling from the same haphazard set.
The same girls, with the sun in their eyes and
the rolling sea in their hips, kissed you
in dreams, in reality. You
baptized yourself in the same river
they blessed babies in; supplicated
to the same sea in which they found reverie
and a salt healing.
You looked down the same mountain
and thanked the island
for a mountain to look down from;
a mountain to look up to, a mountain
to run to. You cried in your sleep
for a country like the one lost sheep,
but said nothing, 'cause you knew chastisement
and reproach from your own. You knew
the music would lull them,
like Papa knew; it is religion
borne from a drumming womb.

Momma knows too.
So parades, parades, let the music
be their freedom. The cadence music,
the calypso music, the soca

music, the kaiso music, the reggae
music, the pop music, the reggae-pop music.

And the reggae pop king sings; *God
is a woman* on the campaign trail;
the waddling seals squeal, the dutchpots clang.

You said nothing, for you were the child
in the new uniform of a country
– cowed by the blow horn;
the blasting P.A. system.

You knew the music – what it does.

And I can't find a name for that look
on the faces of the electorate
in the trance of music.

SEPTEMBER 11, 1987

They killed Peter Tosh
and there was blood
on the TV floor;
when I close my eyes,
when I look through the window.

They killed the radio jock
Free I with Tosh,
and fear was my ally,
looking out through the window
to the yard,
where any minute a gunman could come.

There is no Bob,
no Peter, no Free I.

They're coming to kill us
– the reggae lovers;
the ites, green and gold
friendship-band wearers
with the radio dialled to an island
lingua and a one-drop, cool-breeze,
Stepping Razor, reggae beat.

KINGSTON BLUES

Flying plastic bags,
murals of dead dons,
"No Pissing", "No Dumping" signs;
garbage, sewer water and weed –
the poor man's Prozac – cologne the air.
And there's malaria.
What century is this?

The cactus bites
and Trench Town is
what it was: a place
where children know
how to starve
and women weep.

Somewhere else, maybe,
they would have been in
a museum of the time before
"The Prophet" made it big,
where these children and women
would be waxwork figures only.

THE DANCE: 1986

Jerk smoke, expectation
– the scent of the night.
The big box booms
and the stars wash their faces
to stay up for the dance.

The Cool and Deadly Queen reigns
in the court. Her red, riding hips
rub and dub
the man who wines her on the wall,
the trunk of a tree

– oblivious.

Young eyes steal from sleep
to let it in –
one drop
dancehall,
creation, in the skin.

Ms. Cherry
in a corner
slow pumping.

THE DANCE: 2006

It threads the air like a kite unnerved.
It envelops this Saturday night
dance at Tavern where men nurse guns
and Guinness, shifting their weight
from foot to foot and eyes up and down the street.

There's a room spray-painted with blood
that hasn't been rented in weeks;
you pass there to go to the toilet.

The blue convoy comes
with its blinking like a warning.
The dance pauses,
men stash their weed and guns
into stalls, into car bonnets,
and slink back into the black.

When the convoy leaves,
the dance swings
back to waiting.

THE GIRL & THE HIBISCUS

A girl wears a hibiscus
in her hair, and walks up the road
in Jointwood District with a swirl of dreams.

There's a boy glued to her ear,
and like in the days of her mother,
boys go for girls who wear hibiscus.

And if he keeps fondling the petals,
she'll wear the stigma,
not childlike on her nose

but like your own child mother;
like Hester in the *Scarlet Letter*;
like the sea of children mothers.

THE WOMEN IN WHITE

...are no virgins, but women who know
to wear their white in the dark
heart of a Caribbean night
teeming with the fretwork
of dried tears, sour milk
and some empty nights;
women who meet the dirt-mingled sweat
of their lovers
in full white.

MARCIA

Fat, squat Marcia
sits on the verandah, or the stone-
wall thing passing as a verandah,
with a headache – a la rum cream,
and other spirits she nursed last night –
when some woman answer fi 'ar man phone.

Is not that Jamaican woman calm
when it come to these things.
Is not that we sit with a headache
and bleach with rum, over a cock,
for Marcia, as soon as boss man gone,
fly straight up the yard, to rass up the woman.

THE OLEANDERS

If they were humans
they'd die of cancer;

black stalks of soot,
wilted petals with a shadow of
the famous oleander aroma.

These should have been the crown
of Tom Redcam Drive – hip-swinging women
causing vehicles to collide,
but instead are billboards
of the grime of Kingston;

the snapshot depicting an affected after.

FRIDAY NIGHT: KINGSTON

The beige people go to the cocktail
and pretend.
The men suck the ganja spliff in the yard
and stare
as the music plays:
Now is not the time to sleep, or turn the other cheek...

On the street, while some people sleep,
Cleopatra bags a husband;
the watchmen doze
and a head slams dead on black asphalt and leaks
as cheap rum runs the rounds in the corner bar.

KINGSTON

I

Friday night: and
you, who never got paid,
observe midnight to ruminate
on the Madonna, with child,
the friend who bamboozled you,

and just as him pass, hailing you,
that was it –
you *dig him up.*

II

After rain, a man –
something tucked underarm –
walks, head low like Atlas
bearing the world of the downtrodden.
A fast car, sleek shaped,
silver like mercury,
serves him a puddle.

And the driver, a hyena,
slaps knee and laughs.

ON THE WAY TO HELLSHIRE

There's a man on Molynes, a small man
with a muzzle, like Hannibal Lecter
and the eyes of a berserk soldier.

If these things matter, he'll stay

as you regard the sun at Hellshire;
as you scan the horizon,
the approaching surf.
He'll stay, as you imbibe the Sunday beach
before the lent of week.

And as you listen for the sea cotton's groan
when the wind disturbs her;
as you observe the fisherman sea bound –
a daughter in the bow –

you'll chew on this version of Hannibal
Lecter fixing Molynes
with the other Hannibal's berserk eyes.

ROSE

"Light flushed its crimson like an obscene rose."
— Derek Walcott, *Another Life*

You were statuesque, above the rest in stilettos,
perfect punctuation, innuendos:
Rose who swirled to a love
that one day slowed to a betrayer's metronome.

Oh why didn't you make from those strewn petals
a new ground-sweeping, head-turning,
crimson gown so dazzling,
he, not you, would be the one

these three decades snaking traffic
from Liguanea to Molynes, begging
with perfect punctuation, innuendos,
a head of grey, and arthritic bones!

SCARFACE

is the hero on the walls
of the shotballer stars'
thug mansions in America;
the hero of the dancehall lyricist
chanting the story of the don man
rising from the gully banks in Jamaica;

the hard-faced reject of the revolution
who plots his glory
while sipping champagne that overflows
like rivers of money;
is the don for de likkle man
born from not'ing;
the reality from which the DJs chant.

Scarface is the little man who plots big
in the vacuum of Freedom Town,
Jones Town, August Town, Trench Town,
to sock it to the communist,
to beat de shitstim
and live an American capitalist;
a Jamaican don,
with no nightmares of guilt,

till some small axe
chops him down
and we say goodnight to the bad guy:

a common man
with uneven Justice tailing his back.

STAR INTERVIEWS ANDRE BROWN

She wear dem black shoes to work every day
to play modda to two girls I never meet.

I wait for 'ar to come home to mi
an' de zinc room where wi sleep

with the snake in wi bellies,
till mawning bring one more empty day

an' I walk to school,
sell de rubber bands ah fin'

fo' de sling shot de boys play shooting wit';
fo' de rope de girls twist and skip.

At fourteen, ah look fi mine on de street.
She go church,

come home from work wit' stories
of two sistas inna exam;

in college;
at home, waiting.

An' I carry home mutton,
hook up cable,

an' she pray fi' mi
on 'ar knees.

Last year ah move 'ar up,
out a de zinc room.

An' last year de bwoy
dem hol' I.

III

The voice is, as it were, a struggle between the verb
and the absent tense.
 – Joseph Brodsky, in *Soho*

BEACH SYMPHONY

Each day that the gods sit robed in blue
in the sky, the sea gull skims the ocean
and the sea wind sings.

The bleached sand is packed smooth
as a new road
and the waves thunder in, as before.

The sea-cliff stands behind the girl
who rides the white horse
past the water boys on the bench

and the two building castles in the sand,
who learn today that sand
castles go back to sand.

SHE'S GOT HER TICKET

She's going to skip this world
for the one where the same day won't
bore in and out of her like nothing;
where there are no two
hungry lackeys in politics,
or plain narratives.

She will have an affair
where she will not want to blink
and miss the excited crisis
of two love-crossed stars in silver heat
or another planet rising
from the womb of this.

SHACKLED IN 97

for Lloyd Rodney

Was like flashback
an' braps, memory jus elapse
to de fus time
dem dash chain pon yu han
an' yu fin' yuself cram
wid faeces an' faces.

Yu become yu cousin
on Black Friday,
an yu heart get bomb to pieces
when yu see di tears drop
from de lawyer dem black face,
but none from de Chiefman
wid de hammer han'.

Yu shake
wid de picture: of yu wife
an' pickney bawling each separation;
wid you chain down to de bed.

Si demdoitagain.

It bubble in de blood;
it burn in de head!

MAMBA MUNTU READS POETRY IN THE CARIBBEAN

For Sonia Sanchez

The sea greets me, but I feel too the pain,
let me turn my back, instead of a face
to the sea of the Caribbean.

And the sea echoed
and swelled
as she read.

It pounded
and exploded,
and as her eyes clouded

a poem trembled in my skin
to know the black pearl eyes
deep and calm and agitated as the sea

drowned with this woman
who swallowed the ocean.
And when the time comes,

she appears with
black pearl eyes,
seaweed locks,

and a balm of deep-sea-poetry
for the kin, scattered like
shells on the beaches of the Caribbean.

TRIPPING

For Wayne Brown

I wish everyone spoke in 3D
like my lover; his words breathe.
I wish Plath were a trip
I could take, by putting on
her skin when I want to touch genius
and live
every second.
I wish the wind walked with me;
then I wouldn't need
the fake fan or scents of bottled wind.
Sometimes I wish to die,
and come back truly a god,
to fling myself into the horizon,
to kiss the blue
sky and fly back at dusk,
by the rays of the sun,
the strains of the birds
and the rest.
I wish to be the words for my lover;
tripping like Plath and walking the wind.
I wish we all *knew.*
I wish not to write poetry,
but to walk it; and for this reason
I wish you had never died.

MANGO THIEF

I should warn you

I perform necromancy
on those mangoes you touch.

I spell their seed
to shoot Bombay germ
down the snatcher's throat
through the purple knots of the gut,
to mate enzyme and swim
the red stream, scattering chlorophyll.

Depending on your make,
it should take days to weeks
to sprout some leaves
amidst your earthy film,

to begin to feel strange

eyes and stranger skin.

SEA DIRGE

I

I came to the sea for that age –
old cleansing from all the stars

in my breast; all the drowned ones
from the first quake to the last deluge.

I washed my face in the sea.
And the sea laid it all to rest.

II

I came to her with strong hands
and a steady gaze.

Now I'm a rusting ship,
my backside eaten by the sea.

IT IS NIGHT

when poetry is only politics,
or just prose,
when you hang your art to live
and, next, stop living
to survive; when love
is trampled in the race,
when we cease to kiss the rain
or pray to the stars.

It is night when we breed
generations that wheeze
and call blandness stability
and miss God in the sun.

HERITAGE

I emptied my womb
today; little men popped out
with running mouths, milling lies
like haggling mosquitoes.

A second rumbling;
then swallowing them as it came
was their clone, supersized, in camouflage.
It bared frightening crystal,
ambushed my left hand and took it.

I watched, glued to the corner, bracing,

when, with a rush of blood, glistening blue,
this figure sporting a sheepish look
tumbled out of me.

It absorbed the clone
till it sprouted four heads
with the sheep in the middle
and daggers on its skin.
My heart retreated.

In a vapid voice
it accused me of birthing evil,
stretched one scaly hand in,
ripped out my womb and walked.

THE LAST POEM

The last one will come from the spring of poems
and the pain.
It will come from the green ball I chose
and the yellow plane, instead of Barbie-doll locks
and the tea party.
It will come from the boy who died,
a brother who let go.
It will come from the poems in the books,
the Sunday school pews
and the aunt who taught Jesus.
It will come from the first time I heard Marley,
played by my father.
It will come from you, Reverend Coke,
who preached a tongue that made me think.
It will come from the little ones
who see the fairy soul (in me).
It will come from the man who lives with dogs
on the street; the poor dear I loved.
It will come from every place that was rest:
my grandmother's hands,
the dream of the brown Mother Mary.
It will come from the tears,
the questions
and the throbbing.

The last poem is the fiction of the girl
who walks the dark and light;
the girl with a black mystery springing from her head.

HISTORY
For D. K.

At UWI

your hair was red, or was it yellow spikes?
Didn't see alcohol's love bite,
but your tongue was a cigarette.

Years later

we kept in touch, vaguely, as I do.
It was the column that showed me you,
not the bleached-hair brashness on assignments,
but the peeks at a doting brother, father figure
snatched from your weekly instalments.

Through the grapevine I heard they canned you
'cause liquor was your lover,
or was it the other way round?

At Calabash

passed out, in urine, in a tub,
with a burning butt and a bottle
– a glimpse of what was to come –
a heap of unfulfilment.
I confronted you:
"I know what you're doing – this drinking…
Just write: there's this workshop…"
Who was I to suggest…?

You were a friend dying from not writing –
one of the first to know I was in the family way,
as they say in the black and whites.

The past returns
and moths fight brooms to stay in corners,
like the corner of this cranium fighting sleep,

75

(or does she walk away from me?)
to remember you, my friend
of the bleached, spiked, red-dyed hair;
of the library reading room
– tucked into Lolita;
of the unfathomable, deep hurt:
my friend of the stories unwritten.

ON THE DEATH OF A MENTOR

All the time the river spills,
and the forest is a womb of ferns.

Run to the forest in the dark time.
Bathe in the dew
of the green, dark, womb of the forest.

Let the tall trees
conversing with God,
console.

Find a spot by a root,
like a shoulder,
an arm around you.

Weep if you have to
but hold the years
tight in your bosom

and the ageless fern in sight
and know
all the time the river...

NOTES

"Journey", p. 13: Japo is Cantonese (Hakka) for Grandma.

"Edna", p. 20: Edna Manley, wife of Norman Manley, and considered amongst Jamaica's foremost artists and sculptors for all time.

"For the Mother and Child", p. 36: Pat Robertson, television evangelist in the US, described the January 2010 earthquake in Haiti as an act of God, unleashing his wrath on Haiti for making a pact with the devil prior to the Haitian Revolution.

"And It Don't Have to be Good Friday Noon", p. 42: Legend has it that on every Good Friday, ghosts of the slaves who drowned in the Rio Cobre River gather there. People have reported seeing other ghosts of those who've drowned in the river there as well.

"September 11, 1987", p. 48: Ites is Rasta for red in the phrase red, green and gold.

"Marcia", p. 54: Rass is a Jamaican curse word that can either allude to a curse-word littered "cuss off", or a physical beat down.

"Star Interviews Andre Brown", p. 61: In Jamaica, criminals often refer to police to as "de bwoy dem".

"Shackled in '97", p. 67: "Lloyd Rodney is probably the last person of African descent in recorded history to have been shackled in a British colony." Courtenay Barnett, "Children of a Lesser God", The Human Rights Tribune, April 1999 edition.
See http://www.ar-africare.com/

"Mamba Muntu Reads Poetry in the Caribbean", p. 68: Known as Mami Wata in West Africa, as Mamba or Mami Muntu in Zaire, this is the water spirit, River Mumma in Jamaica, who from time to time surfaces in rivers with a golden table and a comb.

ABOUT THE AUTHOR

Ann-Margaret Lim lives in Red Hills, Jamaica. She has a BA in English Literature and is a public relations media manager within a government ministry.

She has been published in the *Caribbean Writer* (2008, 2009, 2010), *BIM*, the *Journal of Caribbean Literatures*, *Calabash: a Journal of Caribbean Arts and Letters*, *Caribbean Quarterly*, the *Pittsburg Quarterly* online, the Calabash poetry workshop anthology, *So Much Things To Say*; WiSPA's Anthology, *Motherlogue* and the Black Londoners' Haiti Anthology, *A Lime Jewel*; the *Jamaica Gleaner* and the *Jamaica Observer*. She was shortlisted for the 2009 Small Axe Literary (Poetry) Competition and took the top prize (short story) in the 2007 WiSPA (UK based) Annual Literary Competition. Her poetry manuscript, which was an earlier version of *The festival of Wild Orchid*, received the National Book Development Council of Jamaica Highly Recommended Award 2006 and she was the 2005 Red Bones Poet of the Year.

She has developed through the workshops run by Mervyn Morris, Wayne Brown and Kwame Dawes; through advice and mentorship from Eddie Baugh and Earl McKenzie and the writings of greats such as Derek Walcott, W.H. Auden, Sylvia Plath, Ted Hughes, Pablo Neruda, Olive Senior, Lorna Goodison, and others, and life in Jamaica. She hopes to gain an MFA and live completely in the creative world of the artist, sharing it with future (student) writers.

NEW FROM PEEPAL TREE

Jubilation!
Edited by Kwame Dawes
ISBN: 9781845231965; pp. 178; pub. May 2012; price £9.99

In *Jubilation!*, over fifty contemporary Jamaican poets reflect in complex, nuanced, outspoken, meditative, humorous and outrageous ways upon the historical and existential moment of Jamaican independence from Britain and the years that have followed. A majority of the poems were written for this anthology and are previously unpublished. All are by living poets still currently writing. It includes work from the best known poets of the last fifty years, as well as some of the new and exciting voices that remind us that Jamaican poetry is a vibrant and necessary force in Jamaican cultural life. It is by no means the first anthology of Jamaican poetry, but until Jubilation! none has appeared for several decades.

Edited by Kwame Dawes, the collection includes the work of, among others, Opal Palmer Adisa, Lillian Allen, Edward Baugh, Jacqueline Bishop, Jean "Binta" Breeze, Frances Coke, Mel Cooke, Christine Craig, Kwame Dawes, Richard "Dingo" Dingwall, Delores Gauntlett, Lorna Goodison, Jean Goulbourne, Millicent Graham, Sally Henzell, Ishion Hutchinson, Linton Kwesi Johnson, Evan Jones, Easton Lee, Ann-Margaret Lim, Rachel Manley, Mbala, Shara McCallum, Earl McKenzie, Mark McMorris, Kei Miller, Monica Minott, Pamela Mordecai, Mervyn Morris, Mutabaruka, Geoffrey Philp, Velma Pollard, Claudia Rankine, Heather Royes, Olive Senior, Tanya Shirley, A-dZiko Simba, Fabian Thomas, Ralph Thompson, Donna Aza Weir-Soley , d'bi.young.

All Peepal Tree titles are available from the website
www.peepaltreepress.com
with a money back guarantee, secure credit card ordering
and fast delivery throughout the world at cost or less.
Contact us at:
Peepal Tree Press, 17 King's Avenue, Leeds LS6 1QS, UK
Tel: +44 (0) 113 2451703 E-mail: contact@peepaltreepress.com